Walking
On Air

The Memoirs
Of
Jethro Shaw

Dedicated to the family
Of Pat and Jethro Shaw

Jethro Shaw

&

On the Wings of a Dove

Precious Fruit Of the Earth

Jethro Shaw's parents, Howard Jewitt Shaw and Pauline Amanda Davis Shaw

Birthplace of Jethro and James
4-06-1928 and 11-01-1930

I was born Nov.. 1, 1930 on a farm in the Trenton, Missouri area. I don't remember, but I was told sometime before I started school, I had been sick and had run a high fever so I had to learn how to walk and talk again. I stuttered so badly, people couldn't understand me. I remember going to the grocery store and being told to go get a note of what I was after. Before I was sick, I was always whistling.

I was living with my Grandma Davis in Laredo, Missouri. She had breast cancer and went to Kansas City, Missouri to have it removed. She died in 1937 after I was living with my family.

My Grandma Davis bought a wagon for me to play with, that was at her house so that I would want to come and stay with her. When I went home I had to leave the wagon, so I would want to come back and stay with her.

I remember one time when Grandma and I were visiting my folks, Grandma and I went into the timber looking for the milk cow and I got lost. I don't remember how many people were looking for me.

I remember another time, I walked up on a rattler snake. Grandma must have called my dad, for he shot the snake with his single shot 22. Ray Gene Shaw (that lives in California) has the gun.

As a child, I had mineral deficiency, for I would eat the clay from the road bank.

The house that my folks lived in was made from navity lumber, so the lumber dried, leaving big cracks in the floor. Grandma Davis started stuffing rags in the cracks to try and make the house warmer.

My brother James must have had a pet sheep, for I remember it coming in the house all bloody from having its tail cut off.

There was a family close by, that lived in a log cabin back in the woods. He came over to get my dad to help cut a bee tree for part of the honey. Dad's part was in a wash tub. Dark color, since it was wild honey, it still had some bees mixed in. HA!

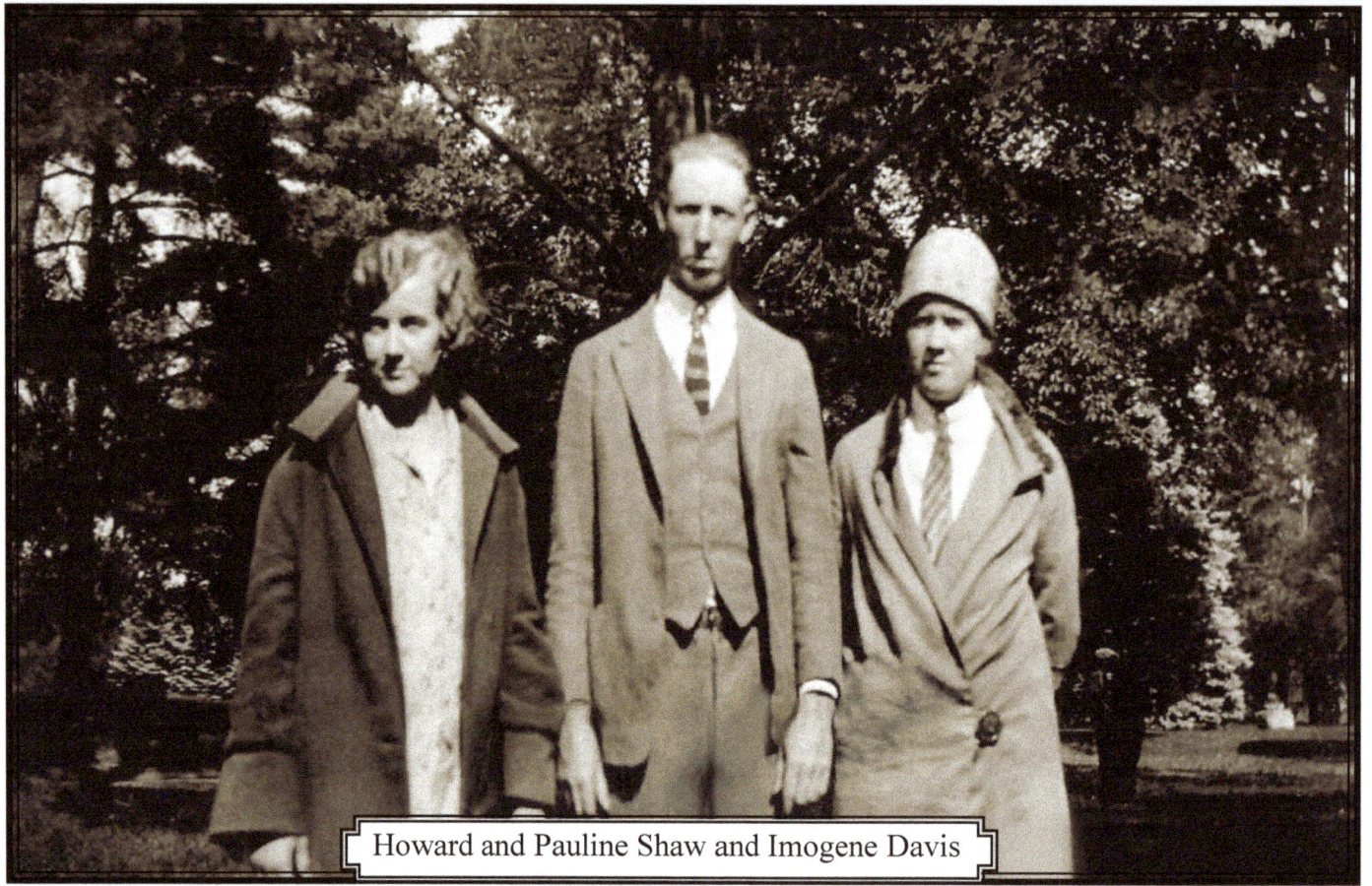

Howard and Pauline Shaw and Imogene Davis

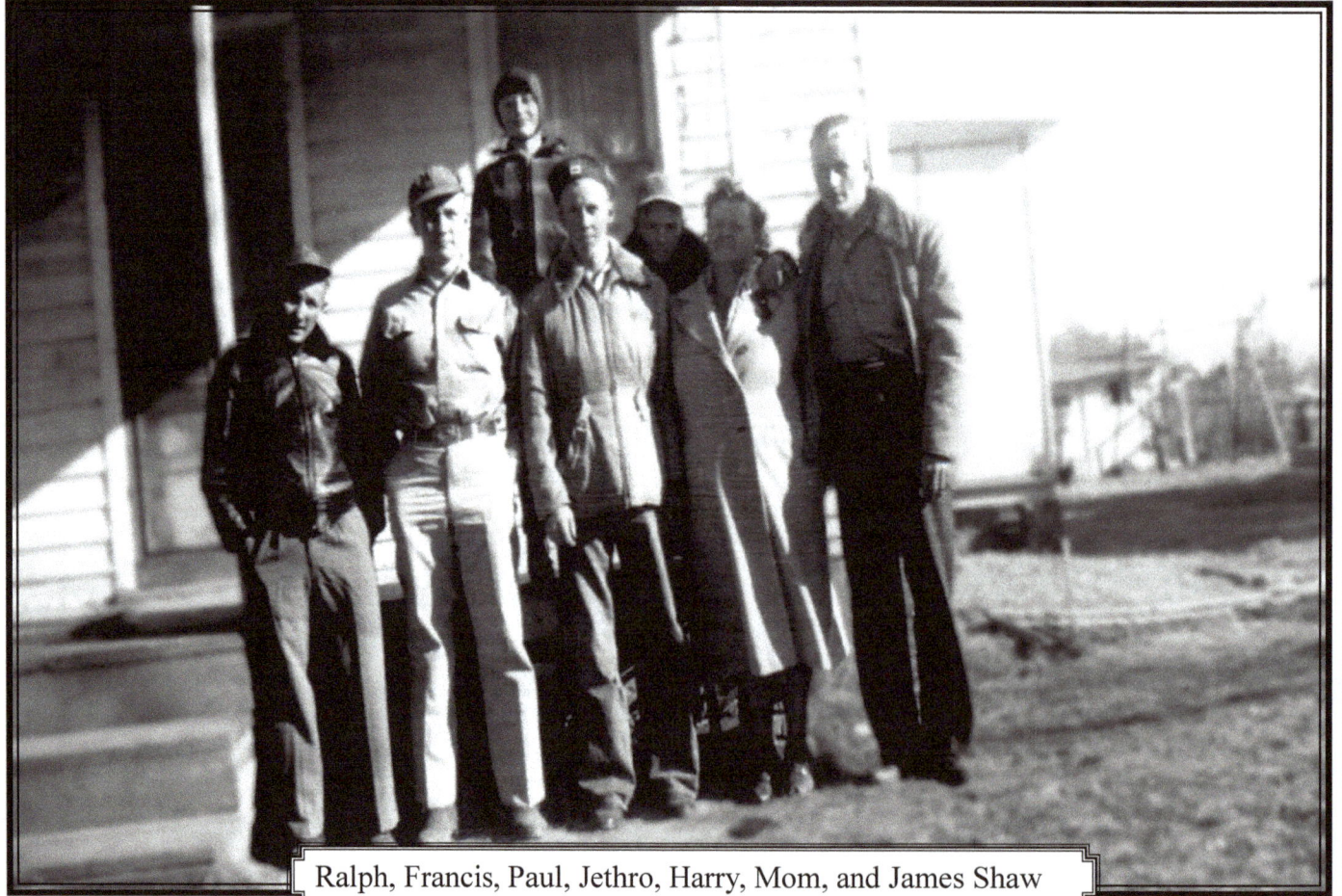

Ralph, Francis, Paul, Jethro, Harry, Mom, and James Shaw

My Uncle Jerome Davis came and stayed to dig a cistern and lined it with rocks that were in the area.

I started school in Laredo, Missouri, but spent most of my time sleeping in class. I would walk out of school. I would head to the city dump to see what I could find. I failed the first grade, with sleeping and walking out of the class room.

For Christmas one year, A Sunday school teacher gave me a metal gas truck that David Shaw now has.

My folks moved to a farm next to a river that we could cool off in. It had deep water holes that fish would get caught in as the water went down. Dad would shoot the bigger fish. I almost drowned in one of the holes. To this day, I start panicking with water over my face. I can dog paddle, and that's it. Hah! No swimming and floating.

When I went through the fourth grade, my folks moved from the farm to Edinberg, Missouri, so that my dad could work for the W.P.A. The men were hauling limestone in a wheel barrow, to the crusher, to make small rocks- to have all weather roads. My dad bought an old truck to help the family income. He would sometimes be gone all night waiting his turn to get a load of coal.

I think it was at Gilman City, Missouri- one night, my dad had a wreck by a one lane bridge. The man in the car was killed.

My dad went to work in the railroad round house fixing machinery. Thanksgiving Day, a crew was moving a pull type grader across some tracks. There wasn't enough ballast between the rails, so, the blade caught and broke a piece that hit my father in the forehead, killing him.

Mom was left with five boys and another due in February. Ralph was the only one to be born in the hospital. I believe her settlement with the railroad was $1500.00. Mom had borrowed $500.00 from her brother. She found a 60 acre farm with a small house and barn 3 miles from Laredo, Missouri. She used $1000.00 as a down payment. A man in the neighborhood told that the lumber they used was from that farm. It was built in 1900.

We had just moved to the farm when Pearl Harbor was bombed.

Jerome and Viola Davis

We walked two miles to Forest Hill Country School that I graduated from the eighth grade.

There was a program that let you get some cows and pay for them from the milk that was picked up every day in 5 gallon cans.

We didn't have any money to pay off the farm, just the interest. My older brother James, 11, was our babysitter (that took care of us 5 younger boys) while Mom worked as a cook in the railroad town of Laredo, Missouri. It was where the train hands ate before they started their run.

We were out of wood to heat and cook. Neighbor men came in the fall to buzz saw our wood to the proper size. I would stay home from school to cut and rake our winter supply of hay. Paul would stay home to help me get the hay in the barn. I worked for five different people on their farms for some pocket money. The summer that I was thirteen, in 1944, I rode a train to work for my Uncle Jerome Davis at Portales, New Mexico, for the summer school vacation. Pat was living with them then. I was paid $50.00 and my train ticket both ways. The only train change I had was at Kansas City, Missouri. Mom went with me to see if I got on the correct train. When I came back, her cousin was there.

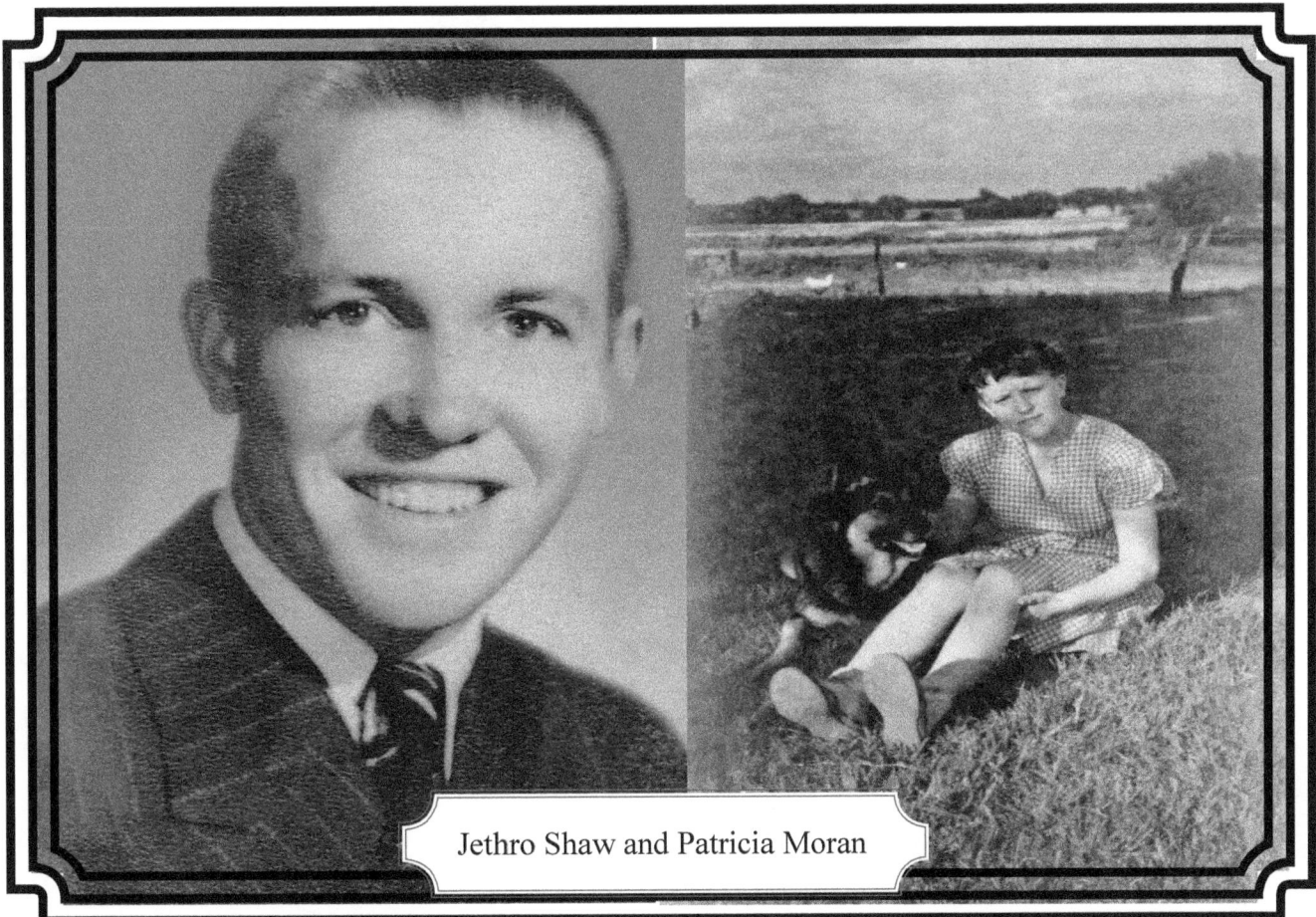

Jethro Shaw and Patricia Moran

Freshman Class 1945 Jethro Shaw - top row, right

Galt School Sophomore Class
Jethro Shaw- third row-last, on the right

I went to the first quarter of junior high and quit to work for the state highway,

I worked with two others, filling in with boulders under bridges that were trying to wash out.

December 1946, James and I went to Chicago, Illinois, to attend a trade school in diesel mechanics, completed April 23, 1947.

Mom signed for James to join the army, he was 16, in 1944, and he joined the paratroopers for the extra pay of $50.00 a month that he sent Mom with our living expenses. He was in just two years.

Galt School
Sophomores
1946 - 1947

Jethro Shaw

In 1945, I started high school at Galt, Missouri. My younger brother Paul was 13 or 14 years old,. (Jethro is pictured 2nd row from the top- student 4 from the left.

Chicago Motive Trades Institute

DIVISION OF COMMERCIAL TRADES INSTITUTE

Certificate

Be it known that _____ JETHRO E. SHAW _____

has satisfactorily completed the prescribed course of training in

Diesel Mechanics

Given under our hand this _____ 23rd _____ day of _____ APRIL _____, 19 48

at _____ CHICAGO, ILLINOIS _____

_____ MANAGING DIRECTOR

J.C. Jorgensen _____ CHIEF EXAMINER

In Chicago, we lived in a basement, with ten, sharing a small kitchen and bath. We worked half a day, and half a day of school. I worked in the sub basement of Goldblatt's Department Store, wrapping Christmas packages.

After Christmas, I went to work in a pop bottling plant where James was working. They also packaged hot chocolate.

When we completed school, April 23, 1947, James went back to Missouri and I stayed and attended automotive school. I soon had to drop out of school since James had helped out with my expenses in diesel school. I wasn't making enough money for living expenses and school.

James went to Arkansas, and made a down payment on 120 acres that was back in the sticks with a two room house. There wasn't even a state road along side of the property. There was a squatter family in the house. The realtor got the sheriff, but they wouldn't move out until James paid $50.00.

While we were waiting for them to move out, we stayed with an old man that lived back in the timber. He had built the one room cabin and hand split the shingles. Over time he had added a lean cover kitchen so not having to cook in the big fireplace. He didn't say when, but he had added another lean to the bedroom that James and I used.

He carried his water from a nearby creek. He wore long johns year round.

James and I soon returned to Mom's, and James bought an old car that had wooden spokes for our transportation. We went back down to the farm that was located between Williford and Ravenden, Arkansas. We planned on making our living cutting trees for railroad ties, and sell firewood for food. We didn't have a car, so we would walk to town, or stop the bus on the main road.

We soon got tired of cutting trees with a cross cut saw and hand axe. The forest ranger had a jeep. He would saw the ties, and he got the slabs to sell for (fire) wood.

James was best at getting 50 cents by the time it made its arrival at Hardy.

June '47, James and I went to Coffeeville, Kansas to join a wheat harvesting crew, but was a day late getting there. James went (on his own), and I stayed for a visit with my Uncle Jerome, that had a farm closed to Tyro, Kansas. My younger brother was there helping out on the farm.

Jethro Shaw

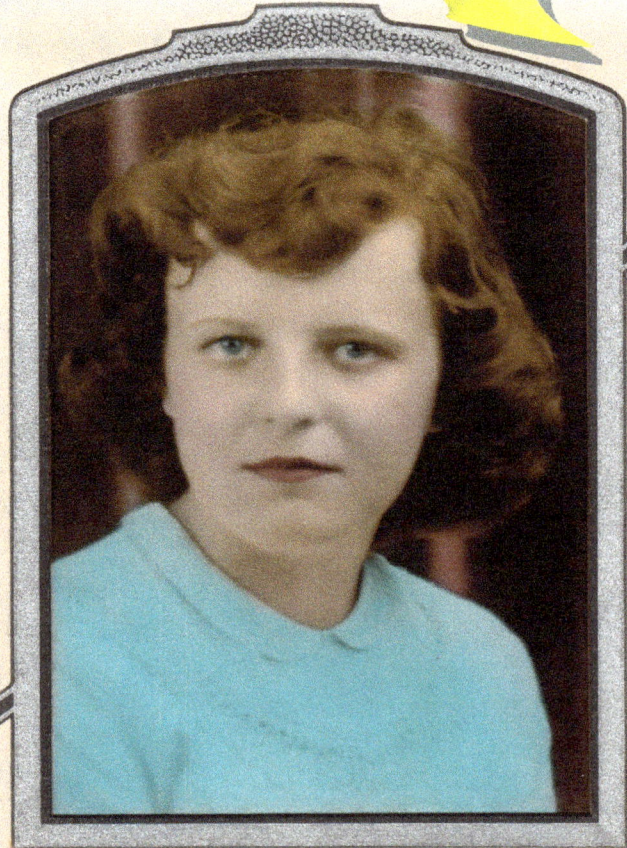

1948   Haddan Studio, Coffeyville, Kans.

Patricia Moran

I went to work on the adjoining farm. Paul wanted to return to Mom's (that was now living at Shenandoah, Iowa). My Uncle Jerome told me that if I stayed and helped with the rented ground, I would get half of the profit.

I went to Independence, Kansas, to register for the service (I had turned 18). A friend of my uncle's- Erney Moran, got married June 14, 1948 in Muskegon, Michigan. Erney had a girl, Patricia Grace who was 13, to stay (at Uncle Jerome's farm) for the summer, then go back to Michigan for school.

After harvest, my uncle told me I wouldn't be getting any money, as it went for payments on all the new machinery.

Paul was working on a farm close to Imogene, Iowa- for Frank Head. Frank Head had a big barn that he wanted to turn into a three compartment building to store ear corn. Mom wrote to see if I wanted the job. I would get room and board $100.00 a month. Paul wanted to work for the nursery as a tractor driver. Frank offered the farm hand job, and still get the $100.00 a month.

In 1950, Frank bought a square hay-baler to keep us busy between planting and harvesting. Then he bought a F-30 Farmall and had a new two row corn picker installed for his farm and some custom work.

I was working 6 days a week, up before the family, to milk the cow, then in for breakfast. Saturday night, Frank and family took me to Shenandoah to spend the night and Sunday with my aunt. I would draw $5.00 in case I needed to buy any clothes. I would buy one pound of candy and head for one of the three movies. I would take in two movies before walking out to the edge of town, where my Uncle Ira and Imogene Johnson who operated the Mount Arbor Labor Camp, lived. My aunt would wash and iron my clothes, special, before going to church. Frank would pick me up late Sunday night.

Ernest and Winnie Moran

Jethro

Jethro worked at Cutty Way
Meat Packers in Omaha, Ne.

After corn harvesting, I went to Omaha to stay with my brother James and work in Cutty Way Meat Packing Plant. I worked down stairs stacking boxes of meat. Some weighed more than I did. I would use my knee to help lift the weight. I would be so tired- at break, I would lay on the conveyor line. I liked to work overtime, to wash down, gather carts, and get to eat supper free. I had to walk by the gut cleaning room. They were cleaning them for stuffing different meat. With the overtime, I was making $100.00 a week.

I received my draft notice that December 14, 1950, that I was A-1 eligible for call at any time. James got married, so he moved out, leaving me to survive by myself. Ha.

I didn't like living in the city, so I went back to Imogene and took a farm job with Dominic Martin, for $125.00 a month with room and board.

Dominic needed someone to take over the farm as he had fell and broke his shoulder. Dominic was a bachelor, and his old maid sister named Margaret didn't drive, so I was the chauffeur. Margaret had 80 acres that I farmed also.

Dominic treated me like a piece of machinery, loaning me out to the neighbors if they needed any help. On rainy days I could go in the house for dinner and then if I couldn't find something to do, I was to straighten bent nails. Hah. I liked Margaret, and felt sorry for her, having to live in the same house as her brother. Ha. I tried to stick it out until I had the corn picked.

The straw that broke my back was, I was to work for another farmer digging post holes for a new fence, and sleep in the kitchen pantry. Dominic made a deal that I would sleep in their kitchen pantry like a stray dog and spend my day putting in a new fence that would require me to dig all the post holes by hand. I quit, leaving him without someone to run his picker.

I went to work for a seed corn company in Shenandoah, unloading trucks from the fields that were bringing in ears of corn to be put through the dryer.

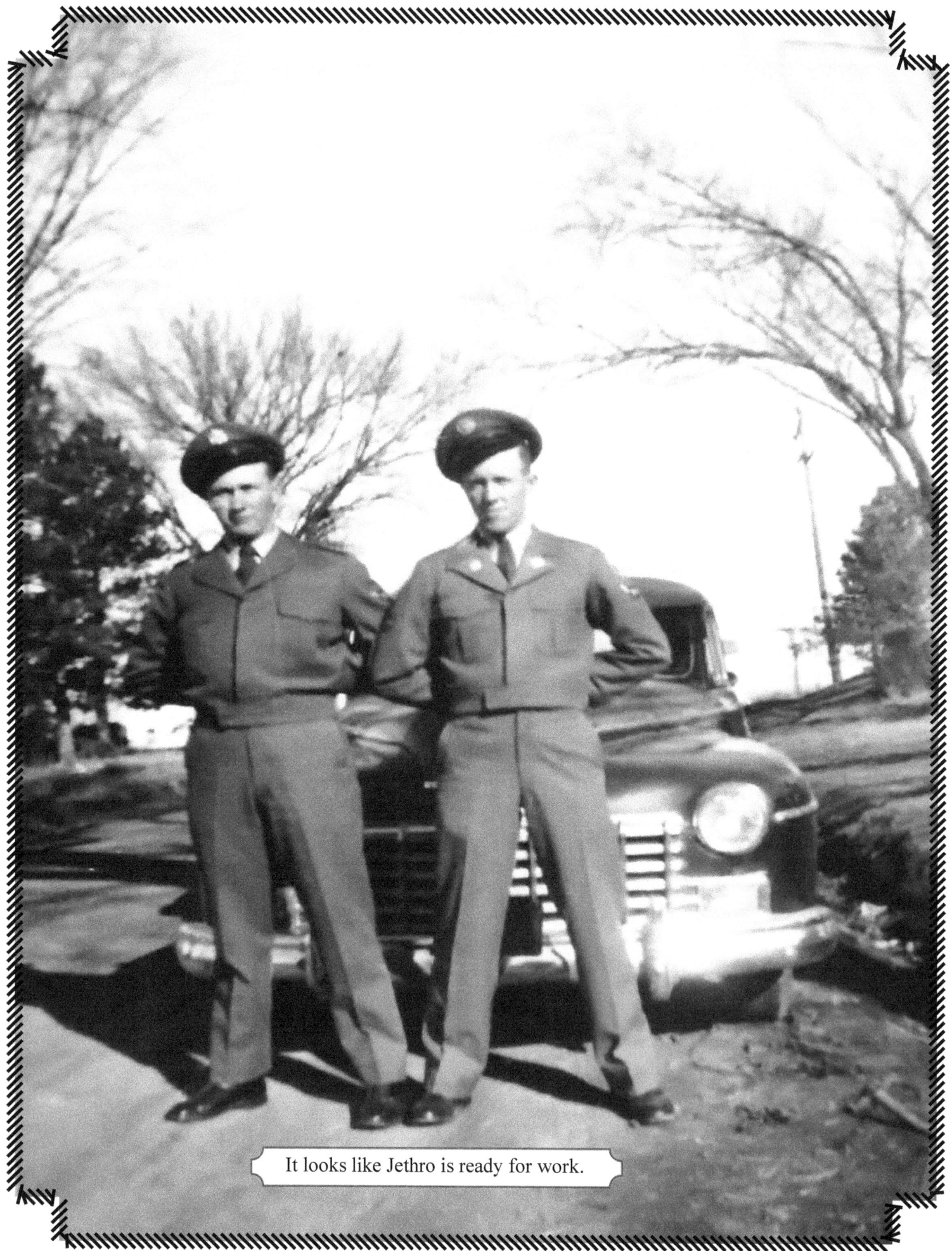

It looks like Jethro is ready for work.

After that job was completed, I went to Muskegon, Michigan to see Pat Moran. We got engaged, November 21, 1951, but no date was set to marry. The ring cost $125.00.

Paul had joined the Air Force and was stationed at Indianapolis, Indiana. So I went to see him and see how he liked being in the service, as he was training for the Air Police.

He said, "So far, so good!"

So when I got back to my mother's I went into Trenton, Missouri and volunteered for the Air Force.

I had a few days before they had an open spot for me to start basic training. I went back up to Shenandoah, Iowa to say good-bye to my aunt and uncle.

I was sworn in to the Air Force December 6, 1957 at Kansas City, Missouri, and went by troupe train to Lackland A.F.B. , Texas. We lived in tents, waiting for room in the barracks. We didn't have any heat in the tent, for no one wanted to stay up all night for the fire guard. Ha-ha.

I don't remember when we moved into the barracks, but I was there when I got sick, so I spent December 25, 1951 in the hospital. I was given a Red Cross gift of four cigarettes and a Hershey's candy bar.

I completed basic training February 1, 1952. My first assignment was Lake Charles, Louisiana, to the fire department. I didn't like the fire department, for we worked 24 hours and 24 hours off. I didn't think it was fair- other airmen had weekends and holidays off, with us working like robots. Ha-ha.

The Air Force was needing aircraft mechanics, and I was one of the lucky ones sent to Amarillo, Texas in February 1953, and completed school June 1953. I took a 30 day leave and headed home to see mom and family in Missouri, then on my way to see Pat Moran.

Patricia Moran
Weds Jethro Shaw

Pat and I went over to see my brother James that was working in Grand Rapids, Michigan, in a factory that made tennis shoes.

We decided to get married, so we went to South Bend, Indiana with her folks to be our witnesses. (There wasn't any waiting time in that state.) We were married June 27, 1953 by E. L. Kingsafer, a justice of the peace.

We had Chinese for dinner.

We went to Chicago for our honeymoon.

I was almost broke, so called my Uncle Ira Johnson at Shenandoah, Iowa to loan me $100.00, to get me to my new base in Alexandria, Louisiana. I arrived the first of July, 1953, and was assigned to the 390th that had the F-34 Aircraft. It was equipped to carry an atomic bomb under its left wing.

August 1953, I went back to Muskegon, Michigan to pick up Pat and a 23 foot trailer she had bought for $300.00. We parked it on the basic trailer court. I think it was $30.00 a month.

I got a job cleaning the bath and laundry house and mowed the grass for $50.00 a month. I used that money to trade my 1941 car for a 1952.
Our first boy, Ernest Eugene was born August 18, 1954 in Pineville, Louisiana.

Our friend Dick Bonderson across the street was getting out of the service, so he sold me his 26 foot trailer for $1,500.00. I paid him $500.00 down and the $1,000.00 when I got my reenlistment bonus.

December 1955, Mom and Paul came down from Shenandoah, Iowa to pull the trailer. They parked it beside Mom's house, while I was going to Aviano, Italy, to set up a NATO base with the atomic bomb.

Jethro, England Air Force Base,
Alexander, Louisiana, 1953

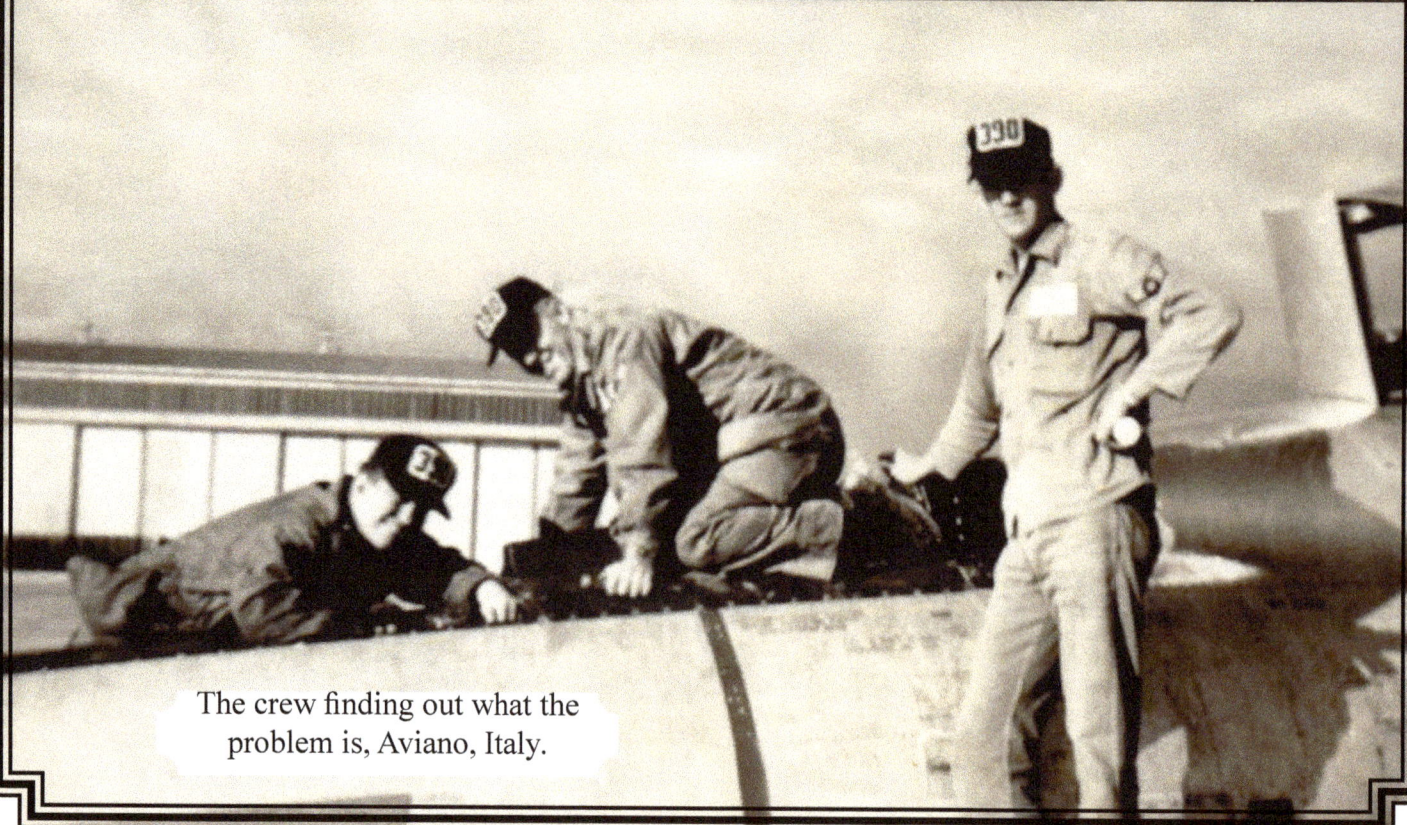

The crew finding out what the
problem is, Aviano, Italy.

We traveled in a C-124 aircraft. Our first stop was Harmon, Newfoundland, second stop- Bermuda, and third stop- Azores.

I was the crew chief of the first plane to carry the atomic bomb, in our squadron, and Captain Tubs was the pilot. When a flight of six planes arrived, four of our planes wanted to make low level flight around the island. First, Colonel Danual's plane crashes alongside of the runway on the grass. Second, my plane with Captain Tub's crashed into a rock fence, killing him. Third, Lieutenant Johnson made a flame out of landing on the runway. That night, we removed and replaced Lieutenant Johnson's engine. Fourth, the plane landed okay. The removed engine was sent back to the states.

We were told that they had gotten some water in their fuel from the in flight refueling (due to the distance, there was being air to air refueling).

Captain Tubs had a boy about the same age as my boy Ernest.

Our next stop was French Morocco; next Rome, Italy; next, was Pisa, Italy- to drop off a mechanic for a repair; final landing, Aviano, Italy.

Jethro in Italy

Aviano, Italy

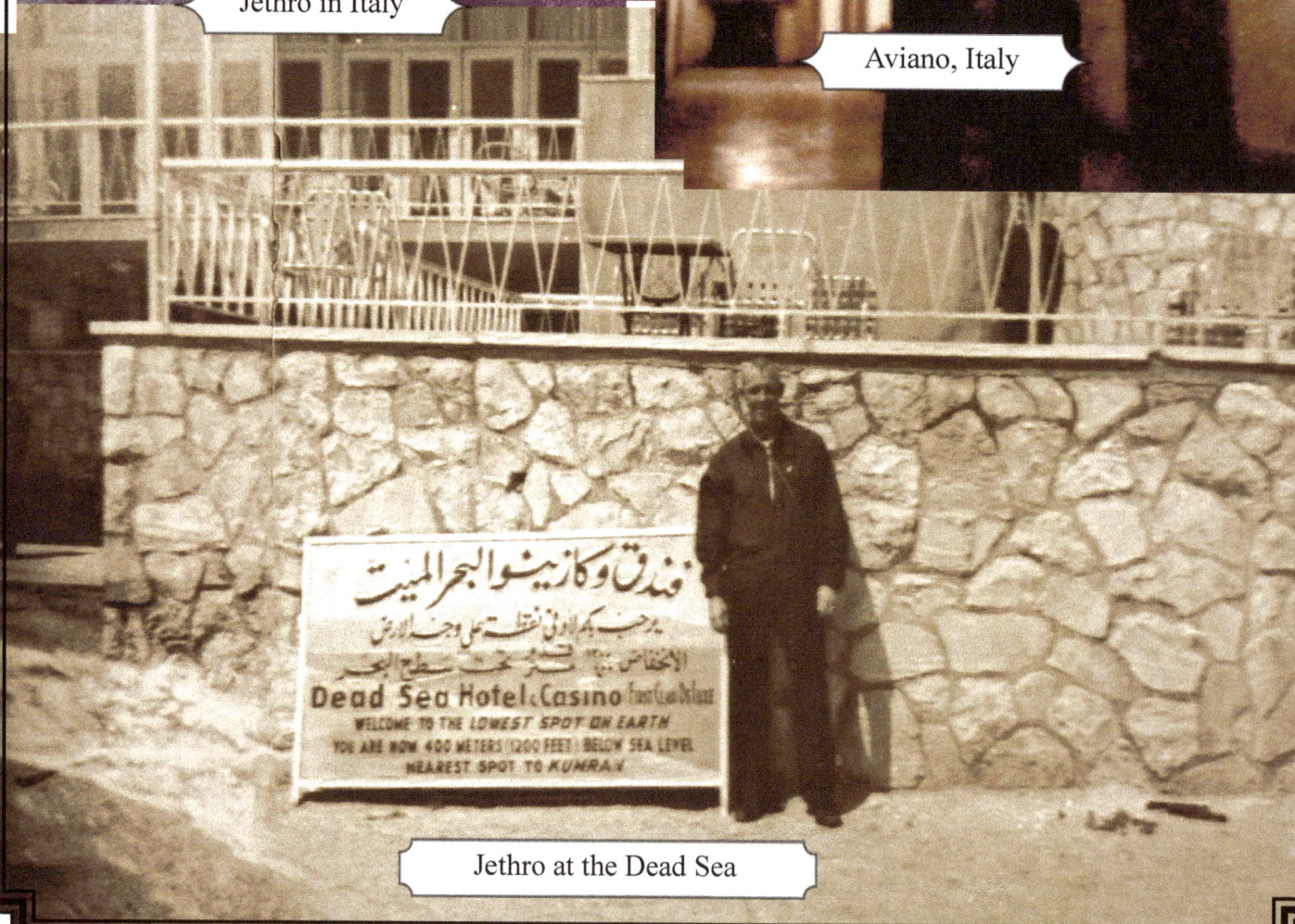
Jethro at the Dead Sea

We visited Venice, Florence and Brindle for Easter. A group of us went to the Holy Lands, the Dead Sea, Jerusalem, Jericho and the other attractions. One night we were having flying exercises and one of the pilots got vertigo, so bailed out of his plane. That made three planes we had lost since leaving the states.

One day, after dinner, I went up in a T-33 aircraft. It wasn't long before he had me throwing up, buzzing the beaches, and doing tricks in the sky. Hah. That was the only time I was airsick. I have flown in a lot on bad weather before and since. I will admit there were times I wasn't feeling so good, when people was throwing up around me. Hah.

Leaving Aviano, Italy, we went to Frankfurt, Germany. There was rubble along the streets for World War ll.

Jethro making a phone call

Jethro working on bomber

My next base was Sioux City, Iowa.

Kenneth Howard was born August 21, 1956, at Offutt Air Force Base, Nebraska.

We paid off the trailer. It was too small for our family, so we traded it in Omaha for a two bedroom trailer.

We lived in the Dewey Trailer Park in Sergeant Bluff, Iowa.

I worked in the maintenance hangar, inspecting aircraft and any other problems like the one that caught on fire. The officer that was over me called into his office and told me I couldn't eat until I found out what caused the fire. I drained the JP-4 fuel so that I could take it back in the hangar to remove the engine. The engine checked out okay, so I began inspecting the airframe and found a bad O-ring seal leaking, spraying fuel on the hot engine. The seal was on the fuel filter on the order of an oil filter on a car, only a lot bigger.

Gary Wayne was born April 1, 1959, at the Sioux City, Iowa Hospital.

March 1960, I was transferred to Richards- Gebaur Air Force Base, Belton, Missouri. It is located on the Harry Truman Farm next to Kansas City, Missouri. We lived in the Olson's Trailer Park. I bought a new trailer so we would have more room.

My job was in the inspection hangar until August 1, 1963, when I took over night duty as flight chief of fifteen T-33 aircraft. They are a two-seater training aircraft.

I bought a 1954 Ford, so Pat wasn't stranded in the country.

Paula Elizabeth was born January 17, 1961 at the base Hospital. David Alan was born May 27, 1963 at the same hospital.

Jethro in Saudi Arabia, 1964

August 1963, I received orders for official assignment to Dhahran, Saudi Arabia, to help train some of their people to fly and maintain the aircraft that was given to them, the F-86 and T-33.

I moved Pat and family to Bingham, Iowa on property that Mom and I owned. That was where a tornado moved the trailer eight feet, spilling all the food she was cooking. Ha.

I drove a land rover with the King's Emblem, so I felt safe when I would go out in the desert to visit and try to learn about their style of life. They lived in tents that were divided, so the women were on one side, men on the other. When I approached the tent, I was to look straight ahead. The sheep shared the tent, so we had calling cards. Ha.

If you were a special guest at one of their meals, you would find an eyeball in your rice. We were told at our in country briefing, to bite into it and swallow. Hah.

We all exchanged unwashed coffee cups. Putting your hand over the cup meant you didn't want any more coffee, so it would be passed to the next person. When I wanted to get out of the country, I would take a weekend flight to Asmara, Ethiopia, where the family of our cook at the NEO club lived. I had a special Ethiopian driver and cart that took me anywhere I wanted to go. He had me to buy the beer and live chickens to take home for his family. He would go to a neighbor and borrow a glass so I didn't need to drink from the bottle like they did.

Jethro, and a camel
Saudi Arabia, 1964

Jethro is pictured here with the truck
he drove in Saudi Arabia, 1964

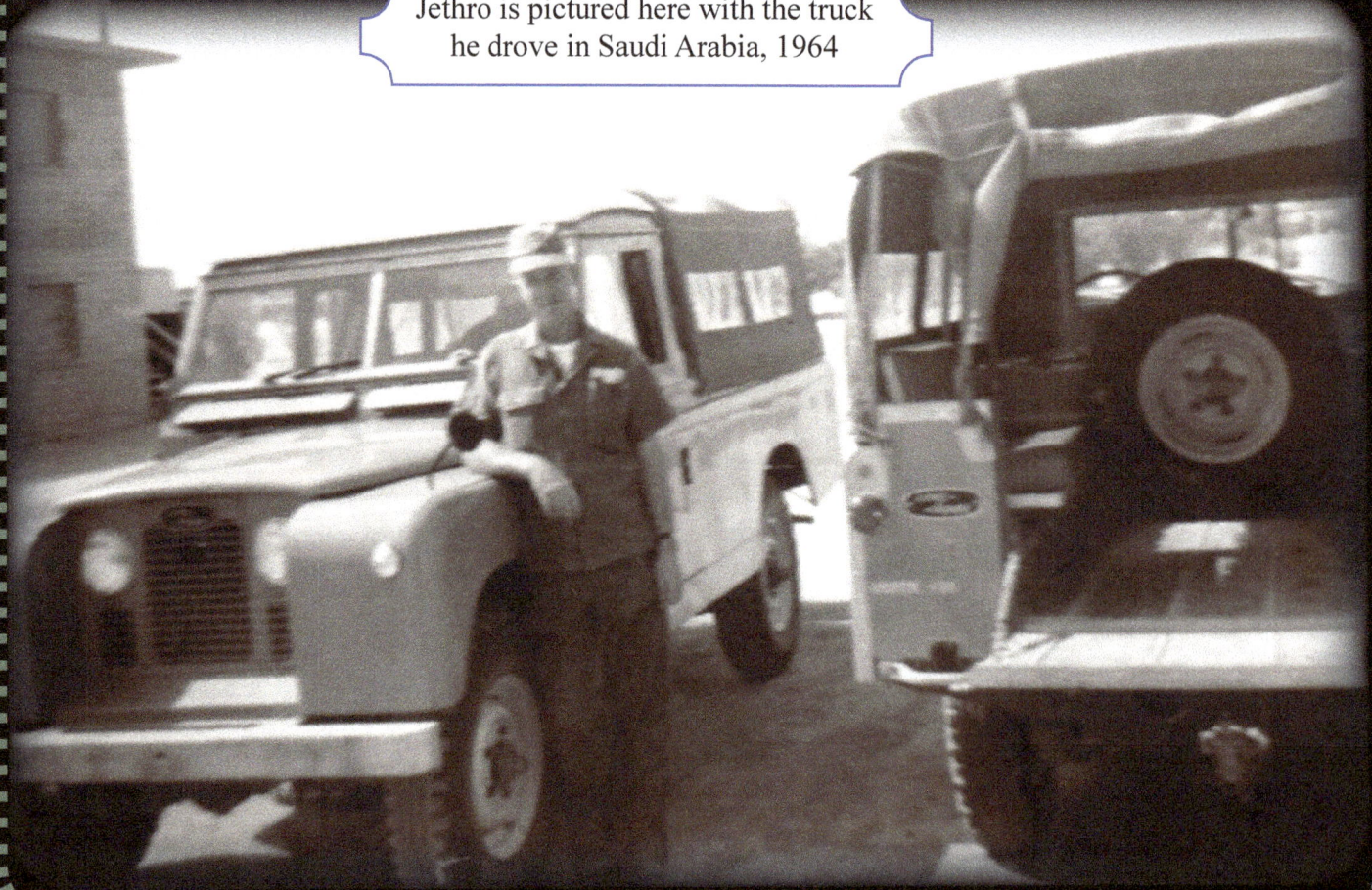

My driver made a fair living, so had two ponies that worked half days. He had added a room on his father's house and even had a cement floor. It was off limits to his little brother and sisters. He had bought a bar of soap for his use.

You walked out back behind a little hill to potty- no building. The chicken was in a large kettle that was placed in the middle of the table. His dad, me and son would reach in for what part we wanted- no plates, nothing else to eat. The mother and children ate in the other room that was a dirt floor. He once took me to the local beer joint to show off His American friend and had me to buy everyone a drink. Ha.

I also visited Bahrain and Tarut Island. It was a long trip to Beirut, Lebanon, where I bought a puzzle ring (harem ring) and ivory necklace for Pat. I brought back a few items from Saudi Arabia.

One time, I had the pleasure of being a guest of the king. The one thing that sticks out was a rice dish that had almonds in it. The king set up front with his doctor and other important people. The doctor would taste the dish that was to be served. If okay, would give it to the king and the rest of us would be served the same. We were to watch the king and when he quit eating, we were to stop also. Then the next course was served. The king's personal guards set close by, keeping their guns in their laps.

Jethro (before and after) dressed
in a thobe, the traditional Arabic clothing

Jethro in Saudi Arabia

Jethro

Next assignment- Del Rio, Texas, we moved the trailer there and had it on base, making it close to work. I had an office position, working between supply and flight line for any problems that needed special attention. Next station … Takhli, Thailand.

November '68 we took back the trailer to Farragut, Iowa. I was assigned as flight chief of EB-66 bombers modified to interrupt the enemy radio and missiles trying to hit the incoming bombers. We lost one of our EB-66 that caught fire on takeoff and crashed, killing all aboard.

I was in the church choir, so we went to Northland, Thailand to sing at a Leopard island to see how they live, not getting to come on the main country. Also went to Bangkok to see the people that lived in small boats going up and down river. While there- I went about 60 miles to U-Thong NW, where they were digging through the ruins. One of the men sold me my Buddha for $5.00. I was told it's one, of the Funan Period, sometime between 600 A.D. and 1431. I have never tried to get it verified.

Next assignment- Luke A.F.B, Glendale, Arizona (next to Phoenix). We bought a house by the base to live in until we could get base housing. It was a headache trying to get good renters, so sold it, then lived in base housing, so made it close to work. Sometimes I came home for a while if everything was running smooth. With the men doing the dirty work (Hah), we would go out to the grape farm after the harvest was complete and get leftover grapes, a $1.00 grocery sack full. One of my workers bought a pickup load of grapefruit. He was a local boy, so had the right connections. Another came back from home in Texas with a load of yellow watermelons. Pat liked Phoenix, but I didn't like the heat, air conditioned house, car, shopping centers.

June 22, 1972

Jethro & Pat Shaw

The first transmissions made at Eaton Corp. were loaded into a Transcon trailer-truck Wednesday morning for a two-and-a-half day trip to Portland, Ore. Dick Brewner, left, was one of three Transcon representatives on hand for the loading of 64 transmission units.

Iowa Western Community College

Council Bluffs   Iowa

This Certifies That

JETHRO SHAW

has successfully completed __36__ months of training in

VETERANS FARM MANAGEMENT

and is awarded this

Certificate

July 20, 1972
Date completed

Veterans' Instructor

Robert D. Loop
Superintendent

James Hamilton
Dean, Community Services

I had reenlisted for another four years until my brother Paul got the job of building the Eaton Plant here at Shenandoah. I had my 20 years in the Air Force, so I put in for retirement to be here when Eaton started hiring help.

My brother Francis had been living in our trailer, so Paul moved it to a lot that I bought. Soon after arriving back, we built a big garage with some of the lumber from Eaton construction. I got a job of putting together work tables and storage cabinets. Eaton hired me November 23, 1971, as their seventh employee, since I wasn't around the day before. My employment number was 7. I worked in shipping and receiving until I retired.

After starting to work at Eaton on November 23, 1971, I tore down houses for the used lumber, then I would sell.

Duane Bredensteiner (south of Farragut) offered a house in the country, if I would help on the farm. Our boy Kenneth was already working for him after school and weekends. I stayed there until I moved back to Farragut, so I could go to study how to farm, since so many things had changed in the last 20 years.

I bought a small acreage in College Springs, for an investment. I sold that and bought another small acreage across from the Hover Ball Bearing Plant, in Clarinda, Iowa.

I bought a fixer upper house in Farragut, then sold the place to the City of Clarinda for future water ponds.

I bought a house on 313 N. Broad St., Shenandoah, Iowa to fix up. That is where our boy, David and family, lives.

Next, a small acreage on J-28, south of Essex… next, a 50 acre farm on Highway 2 between Clarinda and New Market;…next, a brick house, south of Shenandoah on Highway 59- between Beecher Chevrolet and Pella Window plant.

Pat felt like she had been traveling in a moving van. Ha.

After retiring March 6, 1992, we started traveling with the Neihart Tours out of Braddyville, Iowa. One winter we had rooms at Oceanside, California. Another trip: Ontario, Canada, Quebec, Canada, Newfoundland, New Brunswick, Nova Scotia, Prince Edward Island. Several times, we traveled to Branson, Missouri and a lot of local points of interest.

The news article (opposite) was printed at the Shenandoah Valley News Today, which is part of the BH Media Group. June 22, 1972

ANNIVERSARY... Jethro and Pat Shaw will celebrated their 60th anniversary on June 27, 2013. In honor of this occasion their family is hosting a card shower. Cards may be sent to Jethro and Pat at 2019 US Hwy 59, Shenandoah, Iowa 51601.

THE WHITE HOUSE
WASHINGTON

Congratulations on your 60th wedding anniversary! Your support for each other through the joys and challenges of your years together is an example for us all. We are inspired by your remarkable partnership. An enduring love like yours is something to always treasure.

We send our best wishes to you on this wonderful occasion.

Sincerely,

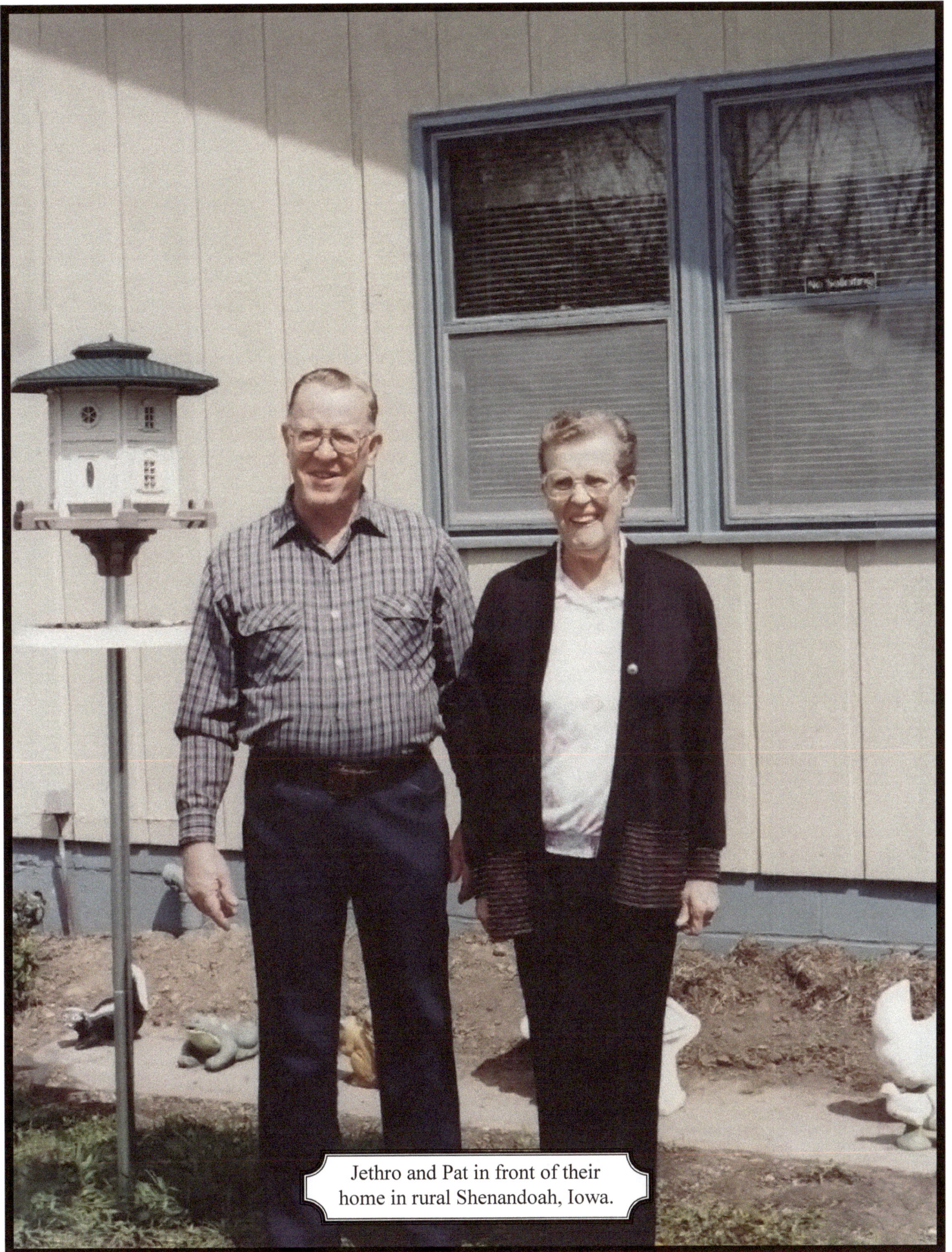

Jethro and Pat in front of their
home in rural Shenandoah, Iowa.

Wrapping it Up

By Karen Falk

Jethro Shaw's military career began Dec. 6, 1951 in Trenton, MO. After basic training on Feb. 1, 1952 at Lackland A. F. B., Texas, he was assigned to Lake Charles Air Base, in Louisiana where he was a member of the 44th fire department, the 1st Instructal 500 and 700 gallon fire trucks. He was a truck driver, and was promoted to crew chief- in charge of trucks and men assigned until he transferred to crash and recovery and was called to assignment in Section Order 3, Amarillo A. F. B., TX on June 11, 1953. Jethro attended Jet Fighter's School, became an aircraft mechanic, and was assigned to the 39th Fighter Bomber. In July 53, after tying the wedding knot with Patricia Moran, Jethro went to England A. F. B. in Alexander, Louisiana and was assigned to the 390th, as a crew chief (1 engine) F-84F that was used to carry the atomic bomb under the left wing that was released and radio controlled to the target. He then left the base to help set up a NATO base at Aviano A. F. B., Italy with the F-84F bomb that would have a different squadron rotating every six months.

While in Italy, he was in Rome, Florence, Venice and Brindisi. On air flight to Italy, the flight crew stopped in Harmon A. F. B., Newfoundland; Kindley A. F. B. in Bermuda; Layes Field, Azores; and Morocco. When his flight left Italy, they stopped in Frankfort, Germany.

During August 1956- Jethro was assigned to the 53rd Fighter Group, Sioux City, Iowa, then in March 1959 his family moved to Olsen's Trailer Park, Belton, MO. There they stayed until August of 1963.

In 1962, Jethro was in the 328th Organized Maintenance Squadron, Richard Gebaur A. F. B.. From Jan. 13, 1962 – July 31, 1962 Jethro was a Senior Aircraft Periodic Dock Mechanic and Assistant Dock Chief. From August 1, 1962 –July 31, 1963 Jethro was the ACFT Mechanic Night Flight Chief and ACFT Maintenance Technician Assistant Flight Chief. Then he was sent to 1141 USAF Saudi Arabia A. F. B. in 1963-1964 where he was a military advisor in Dahran. Jethro drove a truck with the King's Emblem on it. This allowed him safe travel around the country.

Pat lived in Bingham, Shenandoah, Iowa with their children from May 1963 until September 1964.

On September 11, 1964 As Jethro boarded a homeward bound flight to leave Saudi Arabia, four members of the A.A. Bobb family attended his departure. In Doris Bobb's letter to Jethro's wife, Pat later that day, she describes Jethro while on military duty in Saudi as one showing good character and personality, thoughtfulness, courtesy and helpfulness to the many friends he made in Dahran. He enjoyed telling stories to the children, and the children loved listening to them. Jethro went out of his way to help others. He was versatile enough to fit in with the cultured, poised and well educated people there.

Back home Jethro's family- Pat and five children, Erney, Kenny, Gary, Paula, and David anticipated his arrival.

Sept. 1964 - Nov. . 1968 Jethro was stationed at the 3646 Pilot Training Wing, Laughlin A. F. B., Texas and moved to 36 Sagebrush Lane, Del Rio, Texas. While there, he was the Maintenance Verifier Assigned Material Control from July 31, 1964- July 30, 1965, Liason and Verification Monitor Assigned Material Control from July 31, 1965- July 30, 1966, NCOIC Liason Unit at Supply Demand Processing and Research Units from July 31, 1966- Jan. 9, 1967; NCOIC- Maintenance Supply Liason Verifier from Jan. 10, 1967- May 16, 1967, Maintenance Supply Liason Verifier from May 17, 1967- May 16, 1968, Maintenance Supply Liason Verifier May 17, 1968 – Nov. 12, 1968 Then 42nd Tactical Electronic Warfare Squadron, Takhli, Thailand; Flight Chief EB-66 Flight Line Maintenance.

In Nov. 13, 1969- Nov..12, 1970 Jethro was assigned to the 58th Tactical Fighter Training Wing, Luke A. F. B., Arizona where he was the Assistant Wing NCOIC Material Control.

In 1971 Jethro decided it was time to resign from being a technical sergeant in the Air Force, after 20 years. He moved to Farragut, Iowa, in order to work with his brother Frank.

Culture strange, mysterious

Local man recalls 2 years he lived in Saudi Arabia

By PETER WEBER
Sentinel Managing Editor

When Jethro Shaw sees news reports coming out of Saudi Arabia, he is taken back to the place in which he lived and worked for two years in the early 1960s.

Shaw was stationed in Dhahran, Saudia Arabia, from 1963-64 as a military adviser with the U.S. Air Force. He was sent to the Middle Eastern country to help set up a token air force for the Saudi government.

"We were trying to get in points over there and to teach the Saudis how to maintain the aircraft and get them going," the softspoken Shaw said in a recent interview.

Shaw, after ending a 20-year military career, was one of the first employees hired by Eaton Corp. and still works at the plant's Shipping and Receiving Department. He retired as a technical sergeant from the Air Force.

The 60-year-old Shaw traveled the globe during his military career. Here are the locations he was stationed in: Newfoundland, Bermuda, Morocco, Germany, Azores, Spain, Tripoli, Saudi Arabia, Ethiopia, Lebanon, Jordan, Bahrain Island, Tarut Island, Alaska, Japan, Thailand, Okinawa, Wake Island, Hawaii, Canada and Mexico.

Mysterious culture

Married with five grown children, Shaw has many tales to spin from the two years he spent in Saudi Arabia. He also brought back to the States many trinkets and treasures that help explain the mysterious Arabian culture.

One of the treasures is what the Saudis call a "Harem Ring."

The ring means a Saudi can have more than one wife. Shaw's ring is made up of five bands with jewels on each band. The bands come apart. The five bands mean the person who owns it can have five

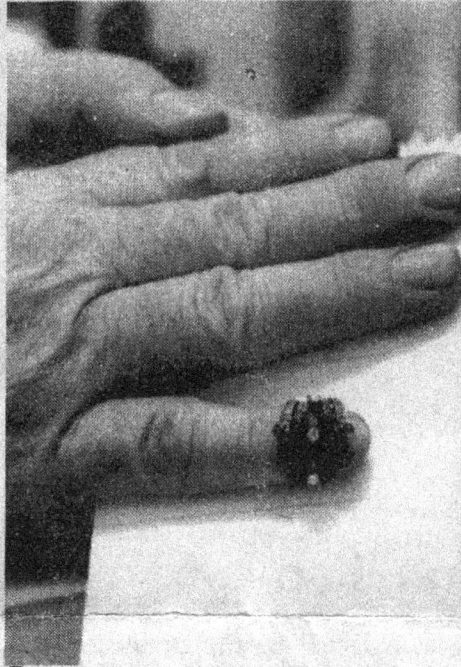

Jethro Shaw (above, right) was in Saudi Arabia 30 years ago to help the U.S. Air Force set up a token air force for that country. During his two years in the country, he collected many interesting items, including a harem ring (above, left). Below are several other times, such as stone statues, bracelets, woman's veil, currency and a rough diamond. (Photos by Peter Weber)

After retirement from the military, Jethro lived in various homes in the Midwestern area. His family lived in Farragut, College Springs, Clarinda, Shenandoah, and a farm acreage on J28/ Highway 2 between Clarinda and New Market. Jethro was trained in modern farming and became certified by the Department of Agriculture in the application of pesticides in October of 1980.

Eaton Corporation was located at 1600 Airport Road, Shenandoah, Iowa. Jethro may have been Eaton's first hired employee, had he been released from military duty one day earlier, on Nov. 22. He made it there on the 23rd of November and became employee number 7. Each year, Eaton's commended Jethro for diligent and faithful service to the company. He had a reputation of being on time, never missing a day of work year after year, for many years. He was shown appreciation by the company members, Human Resources Managers- including Dick Perry, an Eaton plant manager.

Jethro retired on March 6, 1992, according to "The Transmission Edition"- a newsletter that was published by the Employees of Eaton Corporation.

Jethro Shaw's parents were Howard Jewitt Shaw and Pauline Amanda Davis Shaw. Other family members include James Shaw; Francis (Frank) Jerome Shaw- who was born in Edinberg, Missouri, on January 20, 1937 and grew up in Trenton, Missouri. Frank passed away on July 29, 2009; Harry Shaw who passed away in early in 1992; Other siblings were Paul Shaw; and Ralph Shaw, who was born after Jethro.

The Valley News Today (The Evening Sentinel) published an article written by Peter Weber, in 1991, about Jethro Shaw's twenty years of military service to our country. The article states that Jethro had traveled to Newfoundland, Bermuda, Morocco, Germany, Azores, Spain, Tripoli, Saudi Arabia, Ethiopia, Lebanon, Jordan, Bahrain Island, Tarut Island, Alaska, Japan, Thailand, Okinawa, Wake Island, Hawaii, Canada, and Mexico. The article appears opposite and on the next page.

It used to be in Saudi Arabia that a male's first wife was bought for him by his father. After that, it was up to the son to procure additional wives. Today, Saudis no longer buy women, who still aren't allowed to drive cars.

After the first wife was bought, the husband would buy a baby girl who was raised to be his next wife.

"That was the cheapest way to do it," Shaw explains.

To divorce a wife, all the husband had to do was declare, "I divorce thee." Then he is free to get another wife.

Bedouins

Shaw has many stories about the Bedouins, an Arab of any of the nomadic desert tribes of Arabia, Syria or North Africa.

The Bedouins, who travel by camel, wear gold and silver bracelets and use the jewelry for bartering. Shaw said the bracelets were an easier form of currency to deal with compared to money out in No-Man's Land.

While in Saudi Arabia, Shaw would venture out into the desert to visit the Bedouins in their tents, which were divided in half with men on one side, women on the other.

Bedouin men look straight ahead when approaching the tent because they can't look at women, strictly taboo to this day.

In the tent, the males would form a circle and prepare to have coffee. After the "real strong coffee" was served, the service would start around the circle again. If you didn't want any more, you would simply place your hand over the top of the

cup, Shaw said. Guests are always served first.

Shaw has a photo of himself standing beside a truck on which the king's emblem is stamped on the door. That emblem offers great power and privilege to those in the truck, Shaw said.

With the emblem, Shaw was allowed to travel safely anywhere in the country. He was protected by the king.

To give an example of this reverence toward the symbol and what it stood for, Shaw said that if he were out driving around and an Arab wanted to look at the truck, the Arab would approach the vehicle with much trepidation and place his hands behind his back.

Chop off hands

"They don't dare touch the truck because the hand that touched it would be chopped off," Shaw noted.

Arabs believe strongly in an "eye for an eye" and their punishments probably seem cruel and unusual by Western standards. They have little regard for human life, as Iraqi Dictator Saddam Hussein has so dramatically shown.

In Dhahran, around the Arabian American Oil Co. (Aramco) campground, is a big chain-link fence, Shaw said. Any Bedouin caught stealing from the area is taken before a judge, who metes out severe punishments such as lopping off a finger, hand, foot or ear.

But that's not all. There must be "witnesses" to these punishments. So Aramco employees would be

stopped coming into the campground and be forced to watch the punishment take place.

"They didn't have much problem with stealing for that reason," said Shaw, who knew of the witness ordeal and was able to avoid watching anybody get a limb lopped off.

Jail time also is severe. Inmates are given no food by the guards and can only receive it from people on the outside.

Shaw also recalls the time a native girl got pregnant. After she had the baby, the mother was taken to the desert and buried up to her chin. There she was stoned to death. People watched.

You also didn't want to run over anybody with your vehicle, Shaw said. One time, an Aramco employee ran over a Saudi. One of his family members was run over by a bulldozer as punishment.

Also if you are out driving around, if you see someone by the side of the road you must stop and ask them if they are in need of assistance.

World War II brought Jethro and his wife together in unique fashion.

Gen. MacArthur aide

Shaw's wife, Patricia, comes from a strong military background. Her father was on the staff of Gen. Douglas MacArthur and did his map work.

Patricia's father, whose wife died when Patricia was just a baby, had to leave the country during World War II to work on MacArthur's staff.

So he took out an ad in a newspaper seeking someone to look after his little girl while he was away. Jethro's aunt answered the ad and the family went to New Mexico to farm some land Patricia's father had set up for them.

In due time, Jethro's uncle wanted some help on the farm and he answered the call.

"That was the first time I laid eyes on my future wife," said Jethro of that moment 47 years ago. Jethro and Patricia were married June 27, 1953.

For the next 20 years or so, Jethro was globetrotting with the U.S. Air Force and getting to know the often strange and mysterious customs of many nations.

Camels are a familiar sight in the Arabian Desert. Jethro Shaw says you should approach the animals with caution because they're known to bite. (Photo by Jethro Shaw)

Jethro was active in writing to members of our United States government and legislature to express his opinion and views on the economy and the working American farmer, and military man. He received personal letters of encouragement from Shenandoah Mayor Dick Hunt, who is also a prominent citizen, past police chief and magistrate judge; a congratulatory letter from Presidential wife, Michele Obama- for his 60th wedding anniversary; personal letters from President Richard Nixon, and President Gerald R. Ford, Congressional Representative Jim Lightfoot; U.S. Senator Chuck Grassley; and U.S. Senator and Lieutenant Governor of Iowa, Roger Jepsen and his wife Dee- who is an award winning author, was a public liaison to President Ronald Reagan for women's organizations, and founding President of Enough is Enough, an organization that helps the fight against harmful exploitation of children, women and men. (Enough.org/jepsen-dee)

One amusing story Jethro tells of happened in August of 2009. A surprised Pat returned to the house from the mailbox with sympathetic letters from friends and relatives, cards and expressions of bereavement for the loss of her husband. She did not know that Jethro had died. According to one sympathetic soul, the funeral had passed. Pat thought it strange, since Jethro had, in fact, been there that morning before he went to work. The newspaper had published an obituary about another Jethro Shaw, that people mistook to be him.

What an eventful life these two, Pat and Jethro Shaw had and shared together! Jethro and Pat have been well thought of by people in Shenandoah and the surrounding area- for their generosity and their sense of humor.

Although his walk of life began with many adversities and challenges, it would have been a difficult trudge uphill. Having little to work with- such as his own personal resources and his family, and a tool -perhaps, Jethro worked. He worked to overcome walking and talking again, and he worked to overcome when tragedy struck his home and family. Jethro learned how to succeed, even in learning- from flunking grade school to becoming a diesel mechanic as well as gathering much skill in all of his endeavors. He came out on top, literally- walking on top of airplanes walking up airplane runways and flight stairs, and even flying fighter bombers in foreign countries and wars. Figuratively, Jethro came out on top in his lifestyle of sharing knowledge and understanding as well as material blessings to family and friends.

Jethro continues to tell stories of life, the lessons he has learned, and will continue to walk out the rest of his amazing story. Before you know it, he may be walking on air.

Jethro's personal story and military photographs are printed with permission of the U. S. Department of Defense, Book PR Divison.

All factual information presented in this book is sourced from Jethro Shaw's personal notes, photographs, certificates and news articles from BH Media Group, The Valley News Today, as well as his personal testimony. And have been presented and printed with his permission. The information is deemed to be accurate by the publisher.

Opinions expressed by Karen Falk may or may not be the opinions of Jethro Shaw.